Dancing in the Raindrops
A Bedtime Story

By
Ardent Artist Books

AF116055

Copyright © 2025 by Ardent Artist Books

All Rights Reserved.

Book cover and formatting provided by Trisha Fuentes

https://adobe.ly/4aUKuhb

No part of this book may be reproduced in any form or by any electronic or mechanical means, including information storage and retrieval systems, without written permission from the author, except for the use of brief quotations in a book review.

ISBN: 979-8-3484-4489-1 (Paperback)

Lucy loved the rain. While other children rushed inside when gray clouds appeared, Lucy would put on her yellow rainboots, grab her pink polka-dot umbrella, and skip outside to play.

On one particular lovely spring morning, Lucy woke up to the gentle pat-pat-pat of raindrops on her window.

She jumped out of bed with a smile on her face that stretched from ear to ear.

"Mommy! It's raining!" she called out excitedly, already pulling out her favorite rainboots from the closet. "Mommy! I want to go outside!"

"OK," her mother said, "But you have to put on your raincoat." Her mother helped her into her little yellow raincoat and handed her the umbrella.

"Stay where I can see you from the kitchen window, sweetheart," she reminded Lucy with a warm smile.

Lucy nodded and stepped out onto the front porch. The air smelled fresh and clean, just the way she liked it.

that dotted the garden path.

As she ventured into the garden, she heard a small splashing sound.

PLIP! PLOP! PLIP! PLOP!

There, in the biggest puddle, was a family of ducks already having a wonderful time.

"Hello!" Lucy called out softly. The mother duck turned to look at her, tilting her head to one side. "Quack!" replied the mother duck, which Lucy was sure meant "Good morning!"

The baby ducklings paddled in circles, making tiny waves in the puddles. Lucy counted them carefully: one, two, three, four, five fluffy yellow ducklings, each smaller than her hand.

"Would you like to dance in the rain with me?" Lucy asked the duck family.

The ducklings responded by splashing even more making Lucy giggle.

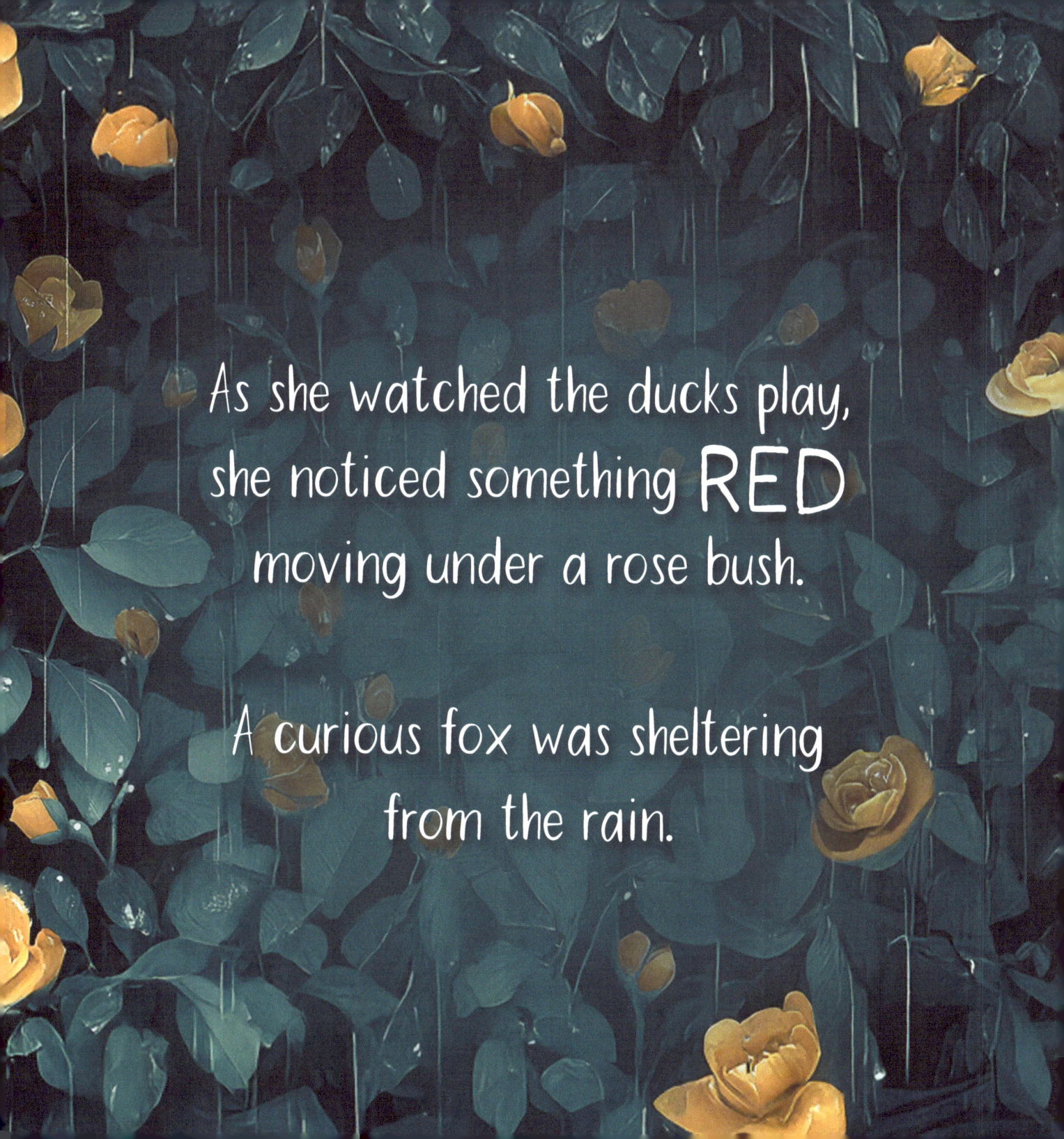

As she watched the ducks play, she noticed something RED moving under a rose bush.

A curious fox was sheltering from the rain.

The fox blinked its blue eyes and gave Lucy a grateful smile.

The fox came out from its cozy rose bush and into the rain to play with Lucy.

Near the garden fence, Lucy spotted something extraordinary!

A group of rabbits were having a tea party!

Well, not a REAL tea party, but they were by the garden fence

munching on wet lettuce leaves that glistened with raindrops.

"May I join you?" Lucy asked politely.

The biggest rabbit, who had big floppy ears and a white cotton tail, twitched its nose in what Lucy took as an invitation.

She held her umbrella over the rabbit family so they could play with her too.

As the morning went on, Lucy discovered more and more rain-loving friends

There was a hedgehog taking a shower under a dripping leaf...

a family of snails were on the garden wall...

and earthworms were doing a wiggle-dance.

The rain began to fall a little harder, making a soothing drumming sound on Lucy's umbrella.

PITTER-PATTER, PITTER-PATTER

It reminded Lucy of tiny fairy footsteps.

"I wonder if rain fairies are having a party up there?"

A rainbow appeared in the sky, its colors bright and beautiful against the gray clouds.

Lucy gasped in delight as all her new animal friends stopped to admire it too.

Lucy felt like she was part of a special secret — that only rain-lovers got to see.

The way the raindrops made the spider webs glitter like diamond necklaces.

How the flowers seemed to dance when the raindrops landed on their petals...

and how all the animals and fairies came out to play in their own special ways.

From the kitchen window, Lucy's mother watched her daughter talking to her imaginary friends in the rain.
She smiled, knowing that Lucy was having the kind of adventure that only happens on rainy days.

Lucy heard her mother calling from the porch. "Time to come in for hot chocolate, sweetheart!"

That night, as Lucy's mother tucked her into bed, she asked, "Did you have fun in the rain today?"

Lucy nodded sleepily. "Mommy, did you know that rabbits have tea parties in the rain, and hedgehogs take showers under leaves?"

Her mother kissed her forehead. "Is that so? You'll have to tell me all about it tomorrow. Now, close your eyes, sweetheart. It's time for bed."

But Lucy was already drifting off to sleep, dreaming of dancing raindrops and animal tea parties.

The next morning, when Lucy looked out her window, she saw puddles scattered across the garden like mirrors reflecting the sky.

And there, near the rose bush, she saw a fox wink at her before disappearing into the morning mist.

Some people say rainy days are gloomy, but Lucy knew better. Rainy days were when the world came alive with magic, and every garden became an adventure waiting to happen.

THE END

Published by
Ardent Artist Books
www.ardentartistbooks.com

www.ingramcontent.com/pod-product-compliance
Lightning Source LLC
LaVergne TN
LVHW071658060526
838201LV00037B/379